PORTRAIT OF THE ALCOHOLIC

KAVEH AKBAR

SIBLING RIVALRY PRESS
LITTLE ROCK, ARKANSAS
DISTURB / ENRAPTURE

Sibling Rivalry Press, LLC
PO Box 26147
Little Rock, AR 72221

info@siblingrivalrypress.com

www.siblingrivalrypress.com

ISBN: 978-1-943977-27-7

This title is housed permanently in the Rare Books and Special Collections Vault of the Library of Congress.

First Sibling Rivalry Press Edition, January 2017

for drunks — ha

ACKNOWLEDGMENTS

A great debt of gratitude is owed to the editors of the following publications where these poems first appeared, often in earlier versions:

Adroit Journal: "Calling a Wolf a Wolf (Inpatient)"
American Poetry Review: "Being in this World Makes Me Feel Like a
  Time Traveler"
Bennington Review: "Desunt Nonnulla"
Boston Review: "Portrait of the Alcoholic with Craving"
Diode Poetry Journal: "Portrait of the Alcoholic with Withdrawal," "Eager"
Hayden's Ferry Review: "Personal Inventory: Fearless (*Temporis Fila*)"
Indiana Review: "Portrait of the Alcoholic with Home Invader and Housefly"
jubilat: "Besides, Little Goat, You Can't Just Go Asking for Mercy"
The Los Angeles Review: "Portrait of the Alcoholic Stranded Alone
  on a Desert Island"
Narrative: "Do You Speak Persian?"
Poetry: "Portrait of the Alcoholic Floating in Space with Severed Umbilicus,"
  "River of Milk"
Puerto del Sol: "Some Boys Aren't Born They Bubble"
The Sonora Review: "Despite Their Size Children Are Easy to Remember
  They Watch You"
Tin House: "Every Drunk Wants to Die Sober It's How We Beat the Game"
TriQuarterly: "Unburnable the Cold Is Flooding Our Lives"
Waxwing: "Learning to Pray"
West Branch: "An Apology"

SOME BOYS AREN'T BORN THEY BUBBLE

some boys aren't born they bubble
       up from the earth's crust   land safely around
kitchen tables green globes of fruit already

           in their mouths   when they find themselves crying
       they stop crying these boys moan
          more than other boys   they do as desire

demands   when they dance their bodies plunge
       into space and recover   the music stays
in their breastbones they sing songs

           about storms then dry their shoes on porches
       these boys are so cold their pilot lights never light
          they buy the best heat money can buy   blue flames

swamp smoke   they are desperate
       to lick and be licked   sometimes one will eat
all the food in a house or break every bone

           in his jaw   sometimes one will disappear into himself
       like a ram charging a mirror when this happens
          they all feel it   afterwards the others dream

of rain their pupils boil they light black candles
       and pray the only prayer they know   *oh lord*
spare this body   *set fire to another*

PORTRAIT OF THE ALCOHOLIC

"The evidence of a successful miracle is the return of hunger."

— Fanny Howe

PORTRAIT OF THE ALCOHOLIC WITH HOME INVADER AND HOUSEFLY

It felt larger than it was, the knife
that pushed through my cheek.

Immediately I began leaking:
blood and saliva, soft as smoke. I had been asleep,

safe from sad news, dreaming
of my irradiated hairless mother

pulling a thorn from the eye of a dog.
I woke from that into a blade. Everything

seemed cast in lapis and spinning light,
like an ancient frieze in Damascus.

Listen to me, faithful silence: somehow
we've become strangers. Growing up

I kept a housefly tied to a string tied to a lamp.
I fed him wet Tic-Tacs and idly assumed

he would outlive me. When he died
I opened myself to death, the way a fallen tree

opens itself to the wild. Now my blood
is drying on the pillow. Now the man

who held the knife is gone, elsewhere
and undiminished. I can hardly remember

anything about him. It can be difficult
telling the size of something

when it's right above you—the average
cumulus cloud weighing as much

as eighty elephants. The things I've thought I've loved
could sink an ocean liner, and likely would

if given the chance. From my window,
the blinking windmills seem

further away than ever before. My beard
has matted itself into a bloody poultice,

and a woman's voice on TV is begging for charity.
She says *please* and reads a phone number. Soon I will

mumble a few words in Arabic to settle back
into sleep. If morning arrives, I will wash my face.

CALLING A WOLF A WOLF (INPATIENT)

like the sky I've been too quiet   everyone's forgotten I'm here   I've tried
all the usual tricks   pretending I've just been made terrifying   like a
suddenly carnivorous horse   like a rabid hissing sapphire   the medical
response has been clear   *sit patiently until invited to leave*   outside the lake
is evaporating   dry blue like a galley proof   a month ago they dragged
up a drowned tourist   his bloatwhite belly was filled with radishes and
lamb shank   his entire digestive system was a tiny museum of pleasure
compared to him I am healthy and unremarkable   here I am reading a
pharmaceutical brochure   here I am dying at an average pace   envy
is the only deadly sin that's no fun for the sinner   this makes sadness
seem more like a tradition   loyalty to a parent's past   I try to find small
comforts   purple clover growing in the long grass   a yellow spider
on the windowsill   I am less horrible than I could be   I've never set a
house on fire   never thrown a firstborn off a bridge   still my whole
life I answered every cry for help with a pour   with a turning away   I've
given this coldness many names   thinking if it had a name it would have a
solution   thinking if I called a wolf a wolf I might dull its fangs   I carried
the coldness like a diamond for years   holding it close   near as blood
until one day I woke and it was fully inside me   both of us ruined and
unrecognizable   two coins on a train track   the train crushed into one

BEING IN THIS WORLD MAKES ME FEEL
LIKE A TIME TRAVELER

visiting a past self. Being anywhere makes me thirsty.

When I wake, I ask God to slide into my head quickly before I do.

As a boy, I spit a peach pit onto my father's prayer rug and immediately

it turned into a locust. Its charge: devour the vast fields of my ignorance.

The prophet Muhammad described a full stomach as containing

one-third food, one-third liquid, and one-third air.

For years, I kept a two-fists-long beard and opened my mouth only to push air out.

One day I stopped in a lobby for cocktails and hors d'oeuvres

and ever since, the life of this world has seemed still. Every night,

the moon unpeels itself without affectation. It's exhausting, remaining

humble amidst the vicissitudes of fortune. It's difficult to be

anything at all with the whole world right here for the having.

DO YOU SPEAK PERSIAN?

Some days we can see Venus in mid-afternoon. Then at night, stars
separated by billions of miles, light traveling years

to die in the back of an eye. *rhyme*

Is there a vocabulary for this—one to make dailiness amplify
and not diminish wonder?

I have been so careless with the words I already have.

I don't remember how to say *home*
in my first language, or *lonely*, or *light*.

I remember only
delam barat tang shodeh, I miss you,

and *shab bekheir*, goodnight.

How is school going, Kaveh-joon?
Delam barat tang shodeh.

Are you still drinking?
Shab bekheir.

For so long every step I've taken
has been from one tongue to another.

21

To order the world:
I need, you need, he/she/it needs.

The rest, left to a hungry jackal
in the back of my brain.

Right now our moon looks like a pale cabbage rose.
Delam barat tang shodeh.

We are forever folding into the night.
Shab bekheir.

PORTRAIT OF THE ALCOHOLIC WITH WITHDRAWAL

everyone wants to know
    what I saw on the long walk
away from you

        I couldn't eat
    and didn't sleep
        for an entire week

I can hardly picture any of it now
    save the fox I thought
was in the grass but wasn't

        I remember him quiet
    as a telescope
        tiny as a Plutonian moon

everything else
    was wilding around us
the sky and the wind

        the riptides and
    the rogue comet
        blasting toward earth

do you remember this
    I introduced myself
by one of the names

        I kept back then
    the fox was so still
        I could have called him anything

LEARNING TO PRAY

My father moved patiently
cupping his hands beneath his chin,
        kneeling on a janamaz

                        then pressing his forehead to a circle
                                of Karbala clay. Occasionally
                        he'd glance over at my clumsy mirroring,

        my too-big Packers t-shirt
and pebble-red shorts,
        and smile a little, despite himself.

                        Bending there with his whole form
                                marbled in light, he looked like
                        a photograph of a famous ghost.

        I ached to be so beautiful.
I hardly knew anything yet—
        not the boiling point of water

                        or the capital of Iran,
                                not the five pillars of Islam
                        or the Verse of the Sword—

        I knew only that I wanted
to be like him,
        that twilit stripe of father

mesmerizing as the bluewhite Iznik tile
        hanging in our kitchen, worshipped
as the long faultless tongue of God.

AN APOLOGY [this poem]

Lord, I meant to be helpless, sex-
less as a comma, quiet as
cotton floating on a pond. Instead,
I charged into desire like a
tiger sprinting off the edge of
the world. My ancestors shot bones
out of cannons and built homes where
they landed. This is to say, I
was born the king of nothing, pulled
out from nothing like a carrot
slipped from soil. I am still learning
the local law: don't hurt something
that can smile, don't hold any grief
except your own. My first time—brown
arms, purple lips, lush as a gun—
we slumped into each other's thighs.
She said *duset daram, mano*
tanha bezar—I love you, leave
me alone. See? There I go scab-
picking again. You should just hang
me in a museum. I'll pose
as a nasty historical
fact, wave at cameras, lecture
only in the rhetoric of
a victim. As a boy I tore out
the one-hundred-and-nine pages

about Hell in my first Qur'an.
Bountiful bloomscattering Lord,
I could feel you behind my eyes
and under my tongue, shocking me
nightly like an old battery.
What did I need with Hell? Now that
I've sucked you wrinkly like a thumb,
I can barely be bothered to
check in. Will I ever even know
when my work is done? I'm almost
ready to show you the mess I've made. I love his endings

PORTRAIT OF THE ALCOHOLIC THREE WEEKS SOBER

The first thing I ever saw die—a lamb that took fifteen
long minutes. Instead of rolling into the grass, her blood
pooled on the porch. My uncle stepped away
from the puddle, called it *a good omen for the tomatoes*
then lit a tiny black cigar. Years later I am still picking romas

out of my salads. The barbarism of eating anything
seems almost unbearable. With drinking however
I've always been prodigious. A garden bucket filled with cream
would disappear, and seconds later I'd emerge
patting my belly. I swear, I could conjure rainclouds

from piles of ash, guzzle down whole human bodies,
the faces like goblets I'd drain then put back in the cupboard.
So trust me now: when I say *thirst*, I mean defeated,
abandoned-in-faith, lonely-as-the-slow-charge-into-a-bayonet
thirst. Imagine being the sand forced to watch silt dance

in the Nile. Imagine being the oil boiling away an entire person.
Today, I'm finding problems in areas where I didn't have areas before.
I'm grateful to be trusted with any of it: the bluebrown ocean
undrinkable as a glass of scorpions, the omnipresent fragrant
honey and the bees that guard it. It just seems such a severe sort of

miraculousness. Even the terminal dryness of bone hides inside our skin

plainly, like dust on a mirror. This can guide us forward

or not guide us at all. Maybe it's that *forward* seems too chronological,

the way the future-perfect always sounds so cavalier

when someone tells me *some day this will all have been worth it*.

DESPITE THEIR SIZE CHILDREN ARE EASY TO REMEMBER THEY WATCH YOU

despite their size children are easy to remember they watch you

watching them   the square root of your gaze   don't forget

how hard it is being young mindless and spitting up blood

rolled out a doorless cage all iris no white estranged from sense

mirror neurons double the pain they see   here is what I have lost clean teeth

god's grammar olives cedar salt   temptation rarely warns you

a useful model unpredictable as an arrow through the spine

its flightpath   its feathery hole   who among us hasn't wished to burst

from our bodies ripe berries crushed under a tongue   for some

to live well is easy   a flea leaps and is unshocked by its flight

for others it's harder and hardly seems worth doing   the better a life

the more sadness it leaves   I do only what comes naturally obey my gut

pray at takeoffs never landings   mostly I look forward to sleep

my body shelved hallucinating tangled wood walnut

blossoms wind near a river that smells like river   it's lovely

because it's simple   just say yes and step into the consequence

EVERY DRUNK WANTS TO DIE SOBER
IT'S HOW WE BEAT THE GAME

Hazrat Ali son-in-law of the prophet was martyred by a poisoned sword
while saying his evening prayers his final words *I am successful*   I am
successful I want to carve it in my forehead I've been cut into before
it barely hurt I found my body to be hard and bloodless as
glass still for effect I tore my shirt to tourniquets   let me now be
calm for one fucking second let me be open to revision eternity looms
in the corner like a home invader saying *don't mind me I'm just here to watch you nap*
if you throw prayer beads at a ghost they will cut through him soft
as a sabre through silk   I finally have answers to the questions I taught
my mother not to ask but now she won't ask them   as a child I was so tiny
and sweet she would tuck me in saying *moosh bokhoradet* a mouse
should eat you I melted away that sweet like sugar in water like once-fresh
honey dripping down a thigh   today I lean on habit and rarely unstrap
my muzzle it's hard to speak of something so gauche as ambition
while the whole wheezing mosaic chips away but let it be known
I do hope one day to be free of this body's dry wood   if living proves
anything it's that such astonishment is possible   the kite loosed
from its string outpaces its shadow an olive tree explodes
into the sky dazzling even the night   I don't understand the words
I babble in home movies from Tehran but I assume
they were lovely I have always been a tangle of tongue and pretty
want   in Islam there are prayers to return almost anything even
prayers to return faith I have been going through book after book pushing
the sounds through my teeth   I will keep making these noises
as long as deemed necessary until there is nothing left of me to forgive

PERSONAL INVENTORY: FEARLESS (*TEMPORIS FILA*)

"I know scarcely one feature by which man can be distinguished from apes,
if it be not that all the apes have a gap between their fangs and their other teeth."
— Carolus Linnaeus

A gap, then,
a slot for fare.

I used my arms to learn *two*,
my fingers to learn *ten*.

My grandfather kept an atlas so old
there was a blank spot in the middle of Africa.

I knew a girl who knew every bird's Latin name.

I kissed her near a polluted river
and would have been fine
dying right there,

but nature makes no such jumps.
One thing,

then the next. America
is filled with wooden churches
in which I have never been baptized.

I try not to think of God as a debt to luck

but for years I consumed nothing

that did not harm me

and still I lived, witless

as a bird flying over state lines.

I would be more grateful

if being alive hadn't seemed so effortless,

the way I'd appreciate gravity more

if I'd had trouble floating in my teens.

Still, I apologize.

My straight white teeth have yellowed

and I can't tell a crow from a blackbird.

I'm sorry. I'm sorry.

This may be me at my best.   Inspiration haha

DESUNT NONNULLA

as a child I wasn't so much foreign as I was very small   my soul
still unsmogged by its station   I walked learning
the names of things each new title a tiny seizure
of joy   *paleontologist tarpaper marshmallow*   I polished them like trophies
eager in delight and colorblind   though I still loved crayons
for their names *cerulean gunmetal* and *corn-*
flower more than making up for the hues I couldn't tell apart   even
our great-grandparents saw different blues owing
to the rapid evolution of rods and cones   now I resist
acknowledging the riches I've inherited   hard bones and a mind full
of names   it's so much easier to catalog hunger to atomize
absence and carry each bit like ants taking home a meal

I am insatiable   every grievance levied against me
amounts to ingratitude   I need to be broken like an unruly mustang
like bitten skin   supposedly people hymned before names   their mouths
were zeroes little pleasure portals for taking in grape
leaves cloudberries the fingers of lovers   today words fly
in all directions   I don't know how anyone does
anything   I miss my mouth sipping coffee and spend
the day explaining the dribble to strangers who patiently
endure my argle-bargle before returning
to their appetites   I am not a slow learner   I am a quick forgetter
such erasing makes one voracious   if you teach me something
beautiful   I will name it quickly before it floats away

[handwritten annotation: "love how messy the words look"]

34

PORTRAIT OF THE ALCOHOLIC WITH CRAVING

I've lost the unspendable coin I wore around
        my neck that protected me from you, leaving it
bodyhot in the sheets of a tiny bed in Vermont. If you
        could be anything in the world

                you would. Just last week they found the glass eye
            of a saint buried in a mountain. I don't remember
               which saint or what mountain, only
            how they said the eye felt warm

in their palms. Do you like
        your new home, tucked
away between brainfolds? To hold you
        always seemed as unlikely

               as catching the wind in an envelope. Now
            you are loudest before bed, humming like a child
               put in a corner. I don't mind
               much; I have never been a strong sleeper, and often

the tune is halfway lovely. Besides, if I ask you to leave
        you won't. My hands love you more
than me, wanting only to feed you and feed you.
        Tonight I outrank them

               but wisely you have prepared for famine.
            I am trying to learn from all this.
               It was you who taught me that if a man
            stands in silence for long enough

eventually only the silence remains. Still,

      my desire to please you is absolute.

Remember the cold night we spent

      spinning on my lawn?

                I wore only basketball shorts

            and a pair of broken sandals.

              I tied my hair back and

            laid out a hammer, some rope,

a knife. What I was building was a church.

      You were the preacher and I the congregation,

and I the stage and I the cross and I the choir.

      I drank all the wine and we sang until morning.

BESIDES, LITTLE GOAT, YOU CAN'T JUST GO ASKING FOR MERCY

Besides, little goat, you can't just go asking for mercy.
With a body like that, it's easy to forget

about the spirit—the sun unfolding over your coat, your throat
too elegant for prayer. I like it fine, this daily struggle

to not die, to not drink or smoke or snort anything
that might return me to combustibility. Historical problem:

it's harder than you'd think to burn even what's flammable.
Once, I charged into your body and invented breath. Or,

I stumbled into your mouth and found you breathing. When I left,
I left a lozenge of molten ore on your tongue. Stony grain-pounder,

sleepy pattern-locator, do this: cover your wings, trust
the earth, spread your genes. Nothing here is owned. The ladder

you're looking for starts not on the ground but several feet below it.

UNBURNABLE THE COLD IS FLOODING OUR LIVES

the prophets are alive but unrecognizable to us

as calligraphy to a mouse   for a time they dragged

long oar strokes across the sky   now they sit

in graveyards drinking coffee forking soapy cottage cheese

into their mouths   my hungry is different than their hungry

I envy their discipline but not enough to do anything about it

I blame my culture   I blame everyone but myself

intent arrives like a call to prayer and is as easy to dismiss

Rumi said the two most important things in life were beauty

and bewilderment   this is likely a mistranslation

after thirty years in America my father now dreams in English

says he misses the dead relatives he used to be able to visit in sleep

how many times are you allowed to lose the same beloveds

before you stop believing they're gone

some migrant birds build their nests over rivers

to push them into the water when they leave   this seems

almost warm   a good harm   the addictions

that were killing me fastest were the ones I loved best

turning the chisel toward myself I found my body

was still the size of my body   still unarmored as wet bread

one way to live a life is to spend each moment asking

forgiveness for the last   it seems to me the significance

of remorse would deflate with each performance   better

to sink a little into the earth and quietly watch life unfold

violent as a bullring   the carpenter's house will always be

the last to be built   sometimes a mind is ready to leave

the world before its body   sometimes paradise happens

too early and leaves us shuddering in its wake

I am glad I still exist   glad for cats and moss

and Turkish indigo   and yet   to be light upon the earth

to be steel bent around an endless black   to once again

be God's own tuning fork   and yet   and yet

PORTRAIT OF THE ALCOHOLIC FLOATING IN SPACE
WITH SEVERED UMBILICUS

in Fort Wayne I *drank the seniors*   Old Milwaukee

Old Crow   in Indianapolis I stopped   now I regret

every drink I never took   all around   coffee grounds

and eggshells   this sweating   a mouthful

of lime   as a boy I stole a mint green bra

from a laundromat   I took it home to try on

while my parents slept   filled its cups with the smallest

turnips in our pantry   the underwire grew

into me like a strangler fig   my blood roiled then

as now   back on earth frogspit is dripping

down wild aloe spikes   salmon are bullying

their way upstream   there is a pond I leapt into once

with a lonely blonde boy   when we scampered out one of us

was in love   I could not be held responsible

for desire   he could not be held at all   I wonder

where he is now   if he looked up he might see

me   a sparkling   I always hoped that when I died

I would know why   my brother will be so sad   he will tell

his daughter I was better than I was   he will leave out

my crueldrunk nights   the wet mattresses   my driving alone

into cornfields unsure whether I'd drive out   I wish

he were here now   he could be here   this cave

is big enough for everyone   look at all the diamonds

RIVER OF MILK

bear with me   it wasn't long ago I was brainless

lazily pulling fireflies into my teeth   chewing them

into pure light   so much of me then was nothing

I could have fit into a sugar cube   my body burned

like a barnful of feathers   nothing was on fire

but fire was on everything   the wild mustard

the rotting porch chair   a box of birth records   eventually

even scorched earth goes green   though beneath it

the dead might still luxuriate in their rage   my ancestor

was a Dervish saint   said to control a thick river of dark milk

under his town   his people believed

he could have spared them a drought   they ripped him to pieces

like eagles tearing apart a snake   immediately they were filled

with remorse   instead of burying him   they buried a bag

of goat bones and azalea   my hair still carries that scent

my eyes   black milk and a snake's flicking tongue

does this confuse you   there are so many ways to be deceived

a butcher's thumb pressed into the scale   a strange blue dress in a bathtub   the slowly lengthening night   I apologize

I never aimed at eloquence   I told my mother I wouldn't live

through the year   then waited for a disaster   sitting cheerfully

on cinder blocks pulled from a drained pond   tossing

peanuts to squirrels   this is not the story she tells   hers filled

with happy myths   fizzy pistons and plummy ghosts

it's true I suppose   you grow to love the creatures you create

some of them come out with pupils swirling   others with teeth

EAGER

a year ago I was dying   purpling like a finger wrapped in twine   my idiot brain

eager as it still is for divinity   nobody noticed my mottled skin   the alarm

ringing *let the dead bury the dead*   faith has rules   that's what makes it

difficult a carnival shooting gallery full of ducks with painted targets

the rifle's bent   you win by not pointing it at yourself

I like the life

I have now   free as an unhinged jaw   but still I visit my corpse and don't know

what to do   seldom have I found something so cherishable   a line

begins and never ends   I belong to his absence   there is so much I need

to ask but he can't answer with my knuckles in his throat   their bruises

their frenzied digging   I pull out a handful of pills   alchemical the body

becomes a mound of jewels   an ancient hunger calls   obediently I answer

PORTRAIT OF THE ALCOHOLIC STRANDED ALONE
ON A DESERT ISLAND

I live in the gulf
between what I've been given
and what I've received.

Each morning, I dig into the sand
and bury something I love.
Nothing decomposes.

It might sound ungrateful to say
I expected poetry, but I did—

palm forests and clouds above them
arranged like Dutch still-lifes,
musically-colored fauna lounging
in perpetual near-smiles.

Instead, these tumors under the surf.

Wildness: to appear
where you are unexpected.

My favorite drugs are far from here.

Our father, who art in Heaven—always
just stepped out, while Earth,
the mother, everywheres around.

It all just means so intensely: bones
on the beach, calls from the bushes,
the scent of edible flowers
floating in from the horizon.

I hold my breath.

The boat I am building
will never be done.

ABOUT THE PRESS

Sibling Rivalry Press is an independent press based in Little Rock, Arkansas. It is a sponsored project of Fractured Atlas, a nonprofit arts service organization. Contributions to support the operations of Sibling Rivalry Press are tax-deductible to the extent permitted by law, and your donations will directly assist in the publication of work that disturbs and enraptures. To contribute to the publication of more books like this one, please visit our website and click *donate*.

Sibling Rivalry Press gratefully acknowledges the following donors, without whom this book would not be possible:

TJ Acena	JP Howard	Tina Parker
Kaveh Akbar	Shane Khosropour	Brody Parrish Craig
John-Michael Albert	Randy Kitchens	Patrick Pink
Kazim Ali	Jørgen Lien	Dennis Rhodes
Seth Eli Barlow	Stein Ove Lien	Paul Romero
Virginia Bell	Sandy Longhorn	Robert Siek
Ellie Black	Ed Madden	Scott Siler
Laure-Anne Bosselaar	Jessica Manack	Alana Smoot Samuelson
Dustin Brookshire	Sam & Mark Manivong	Loria Taylor
Alessandro Brusa	Thomas March	Hugh Tipping
Jessie Carty	Telly McGaha & Justin Brown	Alex J. Tunney
Philip F. Clark	Donnelle McGee	Ray Warman & Dan Kiser
Morell E. Mullins	David Meischen	Ben Westlie
Jonathan Forrest	Ron Mohring	Valerie Wetlaufer
Hal Gonzlaes	Laura Mullen	Nicholas Wong
Diane Greene	Eric Nguyen	Anonymous (18)
Brock Guthrie	David A. Nilsen	
Chris Herrmann	Joseph Osmundson	

ABOUT THE POET

Kaveh Akbar founded and edits *Divedapper*. His poems appear recently in *Poetry*, *APR*, *Tin House*, *PBS NewsHour*, *Boston Review*, and elsewhere. His debut full-length collection, *Calling a Wolf a Wolf*, will be published in November 2017 by Alice James Books. The recipient of a 2016 Ruth Lilly and Dorothy Sargent Rosenberg Fellowship from the Poetry Foundation, Kaveh was born in Tehran, Iran, and currently lives and teaches in Florida.

CPSIA information can be obtained
at www.ICGtesting.com
Printed in the USA
BVHW031934140220
572128BV00002B/179